Koalas growl, grunt, groan, and whine to talk to each other. When a male koala wants to find a female koala, he sits back in a tree, sticks his nose in the air, and roars.

A baby koala is called a joey. A newborn joey is about the size of a jelly bean. Female koalas have one joey about every two years. Once it is born, the tiny joey must crawl into its mother's pouch. Inside the pouch, the joey is safe and can drink its mother's milk. The mother koala raises her baby alone.

A joey pokes its head out of the pouch when it is about six months old. By then, it wants to eat more than just milk.

After about eight months, the joey can pull itself out of the pouch. It clings to its mother's fur as she climbs through the trees. A bigger and braver joey will ride piggyback or on top of its mother's head.

By the time a joey is twelve months old, it does not want to drink any more milk. It wants to eat eucalyptus leaves. A mother koala teaches her baby which leaves are best to eat. At eighteen months old, the young koala is ready to live alone. Koalas in the wild usually live ten to fourteen years.

People everywhere seem to like koalas, yet humans are their greatest enemies. In the past, hunting almost wiped out these animals. Today, Australia has laws to protect them. Koalas' homes, however, are still being threatened, as people cut down eucalyptus trees to make room for more buildings.

With their homes destroyed, koalas are often lost and scared. They have been seen on fences, telephone poles, and street signs.

Koalas that are found in human areas are rescued and taken to parks and other places where they can live safely.

Koalas are a threatened species, but many people are working hard to save them and the eucalyptus forests they live in.

Glossary

aborigines — the native people of Australia

digest — the process of breaking down food so it can be used by the body

gymnast — a person who does special exercises to train the body

herbivores — animals that eat only plants

mammals — warm-blooded animals that feed their young with mother's milk

marsupials — mammals that have a pouch on their abdomen in which to nurse and carry their young

mate (v) — to join (animals) together to produce young

nocturnal — at rest during the day and active at night

species — a group of animals or plants with similar characteristics

threatened — having an uncertain chance of survival

Index